I0811254

MONSTER SCIENCE

THE SCIENCE BEHIND

ZOMBIES, MUMMIES, AND FRANKENSTEIN'S MONSTER

JOY LIN AND VIOLET TOBACCO

Gareth Stevens PUBLISHING

Please visit our website, www.garethstevens.com. For a free color catalog of all our high-quality books, call toll free 1-800-542-2595 or fax 1-877-542-2596.

Published in 2025 by
Gareth Stevens Publishing
2544 Clinton St.
Buffalo, NY 14224

First published in Great Britain in 2021 by Wayland
Text © Joy Lin, 2021
Artwork and design © Hodder and Stoughton, 2021

Editors: Elise Short and Grace Glendinning
Designer: Peter Scoulding
Illustration: Violet Tobacco

Cataloging-in-Publication Data

Names: Lin, Joy, author. | Tobacco, Violet, illustrator.
Title: The science behind zombies, mummies, and Frankenstein's monster / by Joy Lin, illustrated by Violet Tobacco.
Description: Buffalo, New York : Gareth Stevens Publishing, 2025. | Series: Monster science | Includes glossary and index.
Identifiers: ISBN 9781538294321 (pbk.) | ISBN 9781538294338 (library bound) | ISBN 9781538294345 (ebook)
Subjects: LCSH: Monsters--Juvenile literature. | Mummies--Juvenile literature. | Zombies--Juvenile literature. | Frankenstein's Monster (Fictitious character)--Juvenile literature. | Science--Juvenile literature.
Classification: LCC GR825.L56 2025 | DDC 001.944--dc23

The website addresses (URLs) included in this book were valid at the time of going to press. However, it is possible that contents or addresses may have changed since the publication of this book. No responsibility for any such changes can be accepted by either the author or the Publisher.

All rights reserved. No part of this book may be reproduced in any form without permission in writing from the publisher, except by a reviewer.

Printed in the United States of America

CPSIA compliance information: Batch #CSGS25: For further information contact Gareth Stevens at 1-800-542-2595.

Find us on

CONTENTS

INTRODUCTION

Do you lie awake at night worrying about ghouls, ghosts, and monsters? Are you terrified by movies where mummies come screaming back to life? Do you dream that hordes of zombies are chasing after you – desperate to eat your flesh? Or do you dread coming face-to-face with a sewn-together monster that has brute strength and is set on vengeance?

If so, you've come to the right place. This book is here to set out the science behind these legendary creatures. You'll find out just how unlikely it is that: a) they could have ever come to life in the first place; b) they could do any damage. It also gives tips on how you could outwit them anyway.

Meet the Monsters

First up, zombies. No one really knows where the idea of zombies comes from, but according to one theory, the original folklore may have evolved from stories of Voodoo sorcerers (*bokor*) in the Caribbean country of Haiti. The legend says the *bokor* could reanimate corpses. It's possible, though, they used poison taken from the dried skin of puffer fish to make potions that would paralyze an unsuspecting victim. Family members, believing their loved one to be dead, were tricked into burying the body. Later, the *bokor* would dig up the body, "reanimate" it, and convince the victim to spend the rest of their time on Earth working as their enslaved person. Whether fact or fiction, these tales popularized the belief that corpses could be brought back to life, and stories of the walking dead spread around.

There's no doubting the existence of mummies. The world's oldest-known mummy was discovered in Nevada. Calculations say he is over 10,000 years old! His body was preserved naturally due to the hot, dry, oven-like conditions of the cave where he was found – stuck in time and baked solid like a gingerbread man – except, you know, minus the gingerbread.

In the last century, over a million mummified bodies have been unearthed around the world, but it's the Egyptian mummies and the elaborate process of their preservation that have most sparked people's imaginations.

Frankenstein's monster is different. He came from the imagination of 18-year-old writer Mary Shelley, who began writing her story in 1816. Rather than one whole body being brought back to life, Mary's monster is made up of parts of various different corpses sewn together and then reanimated (ew!). It may just be a story, but Mary was heavily influenced by reading about scientists from her day who were experimenting with passing electric currents through dead animals. So ... she might have believed his creation really was possible. Mary's monster was a work of fiction, but could such a creature ever *really* be created?

If a long-buried corpse starts moving again, whether as a mindless zombie, a cursed mummy, or a monster made up of dead body parts, it can only mean bad news. But they are only found in films and storybooks – right? Are real zombies scientifically possible, and, if so, what could you do about them? Could mummies ever really rise from the dead? How could you stop them if they did? And does the technology exist to bring back to life several body bits that have been sewn together like a rag doll?

We'll find out the answers to these questions together, if you're ready to tackle the science of sinister monsters!

Feeling brave? Then let's get started ...

Zombies

Zombie movies and TV shows are incredibly popular. But many things can vary in the fictional worlds of the undead, including zombie speed and the source of the zombie outbreak. Some zombies can run like a regular person; others are portrayed as slow walkers or crawlers. The outbreak's cause can be a natural disaster, a lab-made virus, or it can be unexplained. Two things remain the same, though: the definition of a zombie, and how you get rid of one. Zombies are dead beings who move around with one goal in mind – to feast on the flesh of the living ... and you must destroy its brain before it destroys you.

ARE YOU TERRIFIED OF A POSSIBLE ZOMBIE OUTBREAK?

A bunch of corpses who see you as a free lunch certainly sounds horrifying. But don't be scared; we'll show you why zombies would be easy to defeat if they somehow managed to come to life!

Zombies vs. Science

Zombies fresh from a grave would be slow, bumbling, clumsy creatures. One-on-one, your superior (living) brain would have no problem taking down a zombie. All you'd have to do is trip them up, and their frail, dead, dry bones would be no match for your living, healthy muscles!

Want to know why? SCIENCE!

Zombie tooth trouble

Let's start with what we're told is the zombie's mode of attack: the bite. The only way zombies can really hurt or infect you is with their TEETH, which means they'd have to get *very* close to you and you'd only have to keep clear of their mouth to stay safe. But even if they did manage to get up close and personal, their teeth are not the weapons you might imagine them to be.

When a person dies, the body starts to lose moisture due to a lack of water intake. As a result, bones and teeth become more fragile. Once the nerves in a tooth die, the tooth becomes more brittle and prone to chipping or falling out. Every time a zombie bit into something hard or at a bad angle, it would definitely lose a tooth or two … and you almost certainly wouldn't lose any flesh.

Suit up!

Human teeth, even at their strongest, cannot bite through denim or leather (or a leather alternative). So, in order to stay more than safe against a herd of zombies, you would just need to make sure you cover up your head and neck. Then, put on some jeans and leather gloves and zip up your leather jacket. Complete the outfit with your best leather boots to protect your ankles, and you're good to go!

Zombie lollipop

What's the difference between a frozen zombie and a frozen piece of steak? Practically nothing! And a lump of frozen steak is hardly threatening, is it? If you happen to live in an icy, snowy climate, you can consider yourself lucky; as long as the temperature stays low, a zombie is about as likely to attack you as a piece of frozen meat.

BLUE BLOOD?

A living, breathing human body can regulate its temperature automatically. When your body temperature rises, the blood vessels in your skin dilate (widen) so that more blood can flow to the surface and cool you down.

When your body temperature decreases, the opposite happens. The blood vessels constrict, drawing the blood away from your skin to keep the core of your body warm.

This is why, depending on your skin tone, you might look redder when you are hot and bluer when you are cold.

EASY FREEZING

Different systems in the body work together to maintain a stable internal temperature:

1. The cardiovascular system controls the heart and blood vessels.

2. The respiratory system controls your lungs and airways.

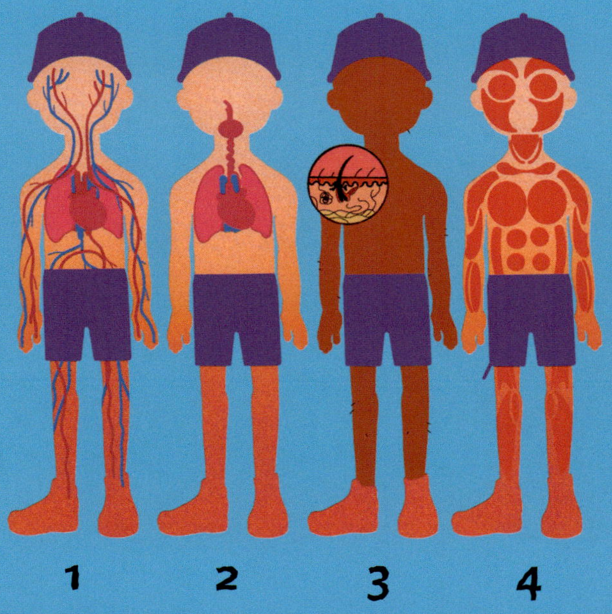

3. The integumentary system looks after your skin and hair.

4. The muscular system consists of all your muscles.

It would be different for zombies. They wouldn't have all these systems to maintain a perfect balance, so their body temperature would be whatever the air temperature is. In a place where temperatures are regularly below 32° Fahrenheit (0° Celsius), a zombie would freeze as solid as that piece of frozen steak mentioned earlier. So if you did spot a zombie ice cube somewhere, you could walk right up to it (you wouldn't even need to tiptoe) and send it back where it belongs.

SAVED BY THE SUN

Even if you live in a hot, dry climate, it wouldn't be difficult to ward off an attack. We know that zombies would have lost most of the water content of their bodies, but under the hot sun they'd lose even more moisture – and faster.

Ever wondered why zombies in films walk so weirdly? Your leg bones are solid and can only bend at the joints, where the tendons help to hold your bones together. The tendons are part of your muscular system. They stretch and tighten to move the bones, which are part of your skeletal system.

Now, forget that frozen steak and think about beef jerky instead. If you've ever chewed on some, you'll know it's tough stuff. Without moisture, dried-out zombie flesh would be just like jerky. The tendons wouldn't work. Movement would be re-e-ally stiff, slow, and jerky. So, if you spot a dried-out zombie in a hot climate, you'll have no trouble running rings around it.

ZOMBIE VOLCANO

If we add humidity to the hot climate, things would get a lot messier. But this means you're even safer! With a combination of heat and moisture, bacteria (see page 18) inside a zombie's digestive system would start breaking down or eating into its body, creating a chemical reaction.

This chemical reaction releases gases, and you can guess what happens when gases get trapped in the body, can't you? They have to find a way out, and they can only do that via a big explosion. Boom! A zombie would turn into a human volcano, spitting out body bits like molten lava. The cleanup is a pain, of course, but as long as you've kept your distance, you'll be safe! See? Nothing to worry about.

STIFF STUFF

Even if you live in a moderate climate, where a zombie wouldn't freeze, dry up, or explode, you'll be okay. Newly escaped zombies would barely be able to move at all because of a condition known as rigor mortis.

Once a person dies, they can't breathe anymore, so they can't bring any more oxygen into their lungs, and oxygen is essential for movement. Burning oxygen produces the energy your body needs to move around. So, when the body runs out of oxygen, it also runs out of energy: the body stops working and the muscles start to stiffen. It can take from four hours to four days after a person dies (depending on the temperature) for their body to go completely stiff – for rigor mortis to set in. So most long-dead zombies would be a bit more like giant walking sticks than effective predators!

CRAWLER

What if a zombie managed to keep moving despite rigor mortis? It still wouldn't be much of a threat. Over time, losing more and more moisture, the zombie would keep getting thinner. Supposing it had a belt around its jeans. Its fingers would be too stiff to tighten it, so eventually its jeans would just fall down. The zombie is guaranteed to trip over them. Falling over is dangerous for a zombie. Remember, its bones are dried-out and weakened, so there's a strong chance some of them will break. With a couple of broken legs and no muscles to help it move, the zombie wouldn't have the strength to climb back upright. It would be stuck crawling around on the ground.

Imagine a herd of zombies running towards you. Scary thought, isn't it? Now imagine them all *crawling* towards you instead ... with their trousers around their ankles. It's still not great, but they'd be a lot easier to defeat ... if you can stop laughing for long enough.

Zombie flesh-eaters

So that's zombies more or less defeated, but there's one last question that really needs an answer. Just supposing a zombie did catch hold of you. Could it actually eat you? It's a very nasty idea, but you'll be pleased to know that it probably couldn't. After all, once a person dies, their digestive system stops working. If a zombie managed to take a bite out of your flesh (and bear in mind how hard that's going to be considering the state of its teeth), its stomach wouldn't be able to break the flesh down into small enough components for its body to absorb. Even supposing the zombie was able to swallow it, the flesh would still get stuck in its stomach and its stomach would be permanently full. If the zombie isn't hungry, it isn't going to eat, so it's even less likely to chase you, right?

Rainforest zombies

Human zombies have never actually existed, apart from in people's wild imaginations ... but how about this? Scientists working on the rainforest floor have come across a strange phenomenon. Ants going about their daily business can be infected by the spores of a fungus, which then takes control of their brain. The fungus uses the ant, in a zombie-like trance, to find its way to a juicy leaf. Once there, the fungus bursts out of the ant's head (ew!) and further spreads its deadly spores. The fungus kills the ant, of course, while its spores go on to infect more of its fellow ants. Could a zombifying fungus or virus one day target humans?

Let's face it – fungi aside – if one ever comes, a zombie apocalypse isn't going to be too much of a problem. Your best tactic? Just stay indoors for a few days and wait for the zombies to collapse in a heap.

ZOMBIE APOCALYPSE: UNLIKELY!

Mummies

Mention the word "mummy" to most people and one of two images will usually spring to mind.

1. King Tutankhamun's sarcophagus with its fabulous gold-plated mask (and the blackened, shriveled, linen-wrapped corpse lying behind it).

2. That game you play at Halloween, where teams race to swaddle a friend in about five rolls of toilet paper.

A WORD OF WARNING

If you're keeping your eyes peeled for mummy attacks, remember: not all mummies come wrapped in bandages!

I WANT MY MUMMY!

In movies, books, and on TV, you've probably seen mummies portrayed as angry, vengeful fellas with one goal in mind: to destroy the person (or people) who woke them from their sweet dreams. It's understandable. If you were dragged from the comfort of your warm bed into a freezing winter's night, you'd be pretty mad too.

On the other hand, witnessing a thousand-year-old corpse rise from the dead and start to move towards you doesn't bear thinking about. Avoidance is going to be your best tactic. To make sure you're never in a position to disturb a mummy, you'll need to know where they're likely to lurk.

BECOMING A MUMMY

The word "mummify" actually refers to the process of preserving a dead body, and that process can happen with or without human interference. When a dead body lies in an environment that lacks oxygen, it won't decay in the usual way. It will mummify naturally – so no need for the bandages. All over the world, natural mummies have been found on frozen mountaintops or buried beneath scorching desert sands, and some particularly fine specimens have even been found in bogs.

STUCK IN THE BOG

Bodies sucked into a bog are preserved with a special natural ingredient: sphagnum moss. The moss contains the chemical elements calcium and magnesium, which turn the water of the bog acidic. This helps to preserve some bodies so well that scientists can see stubble on a chin, the brain inside the skull, and what the person ate for breakfast thousands of years earlier. They can even work out – from a gash in the throat or a dent in the skull, for example – how the owner of the body was killed.

It seems these natural mummies often died very unnatural deaths. So, definitely avoid icy mountaintops and deserts, but especially stay away from bogs, because those murdered mummies will definitely be looking for revenge.

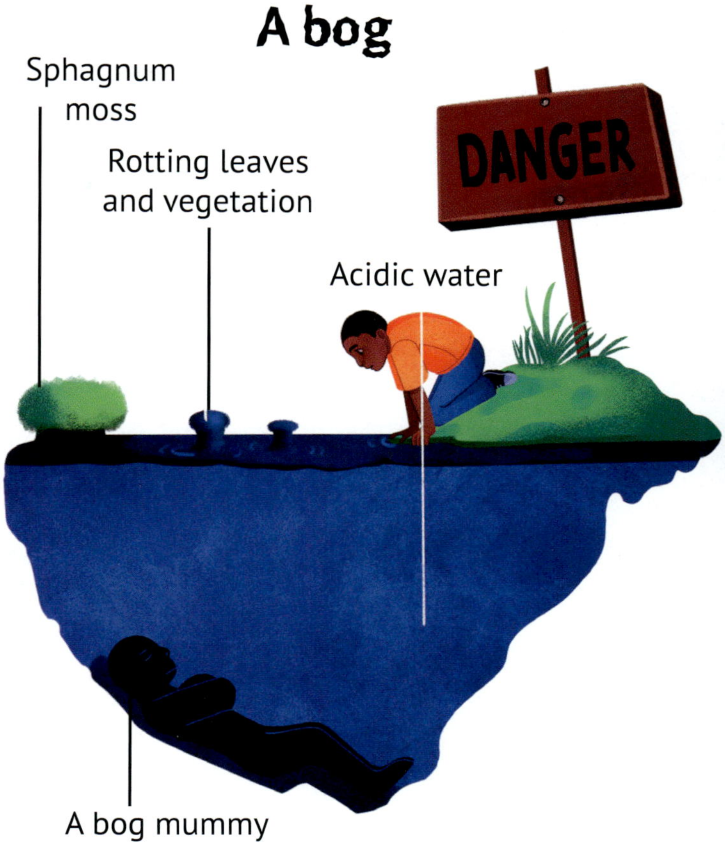

EGYPTIAN MUMMIES

Films usually torment us with the wrapped-up variety of mummy bursting from its coffin and advancing stiffly towards its victim. Human preservation was practiced all over the world, but most of those movie mummies come from ancient Egypt, and they may be hard to avoid – there could be one or two lurking in your local museum!

The Egyptians were particularly good at mummification, and an Egyptian mummy, once disturbed, has extra reason to be angry: its dead body will have suffered around 70 days of poking, prodding, and slicing, not to mention all the rituals and ceremonies it went through before it was allowed to rest in peace. But why did the Egyptians go to so much trouble?

NATURE'S GARBAGE COLLECTORS

When a person dies, blood stops circulating around the body almost immediately, so oxygen isn't delivered to the body's cells and they start to self-destruct in a process called autolysis. This basically means their body tissue is broken down. It's a dirty job, but bacteria are happy to do it.

Bacteria are essential to our planet because they recycle energy. They tackle nature's waste and make nutrients from it, releasing chemicals – such as carbon, nitrogen, and phosphorus – that can be used to build new organisms. Think of bacteria as nature's garbage collectors, taking away your overflowing recycling bins and bringing back recycled paper! However, most bacteria can't survive in certain conditions, and it's this fact that makes mummification possible.

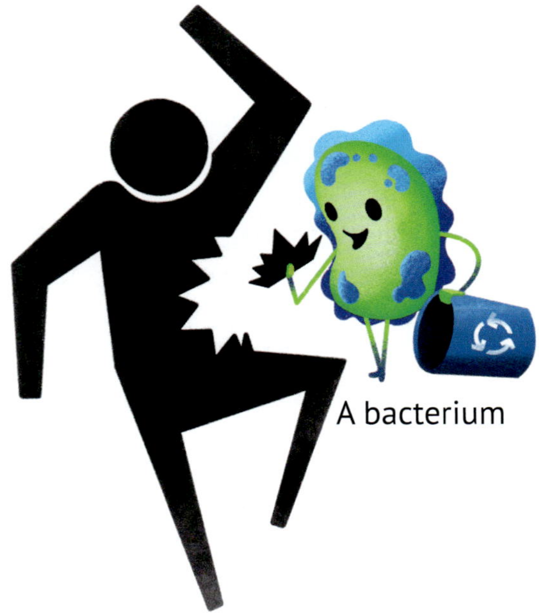

A bacterium

MUMMIFICATION

The embalmers, who carried out mummifications, were basically stopping the natural process of decay. They'd start with the stomach and intestines, because those are the first bits to go bad. These body parts contain powerful digestive enzymes that are usually used to break down food. Once food stops entering the digestive system, the enzymes start digesting the rest of the body's cells instead. An embalmer's first move was therefore to whip out all the internal organs to nip the process of decay in the bud.

Then they washed the body with palm wine and water from the Nile River and removed the brain by slipping a hook up a nostril and dragging it out in pieces. Nice!

The only organ they left in the body once they'd finished was the heart. For the ancient Egyptians, the heart was extremely important. They believed it would be weighed in the afterlife to see how good or bad the dead person had been when they were alive.

STOMACH IN A JAR

The removed organs – stomach, intestines, lungs, and liver – were preserved in four special "canopic" jars to be buried along with the mummy. But have you ever seen a mummy running along with four jars tucked under its arm? If it's coming up straight from the tomb, after it's been disturbed from a thousand-year sleep, it won't have time to pop those vital organs back in again, so it's going to have difficulty functioning without a brain and it'll be very easy to confuse. Run in zigzags, hide around corners – it's hardly likely to be able to find you.

KEEPING IT REAL

The ancient Egyptians believed that once they died, their spirit only left the body temporarily – spirit and body would be reunited quickly if all went well during the Final Judgement in the Underworld (yikes!). In order to receive the soul back and live a happy afterlife, the dead physical body needed to stay in tip-top condition, hanging on to as much skin tissue as possible. It was especially important for the pharaohs (the great rulers of ancient Egypt) to stay in good shape after death, because they were destined to live like gods in the afterlife.

Rich people also went to great lengths to stop their dead bodies from decomposing – the better preserved they were and the more goodies they had in their tombs, the better their afterlife would be.

Poor Egyptians, on the other hand, could only wrap their loved ones in a blanket, bury them in the desert, and hope the hot sand would do the rest.

MAD MUMMY

What if the spirit never made it back to the body? That would definitely make a mummy mad, especially if they'd paid for a very expensive burial. It might even be angry enough to rise screaming from its tomb – just like the ones in movies – before catching you by the neck and attempting to strangle you! But hang on, could a mummy really do any of that? Let's start with the scream.

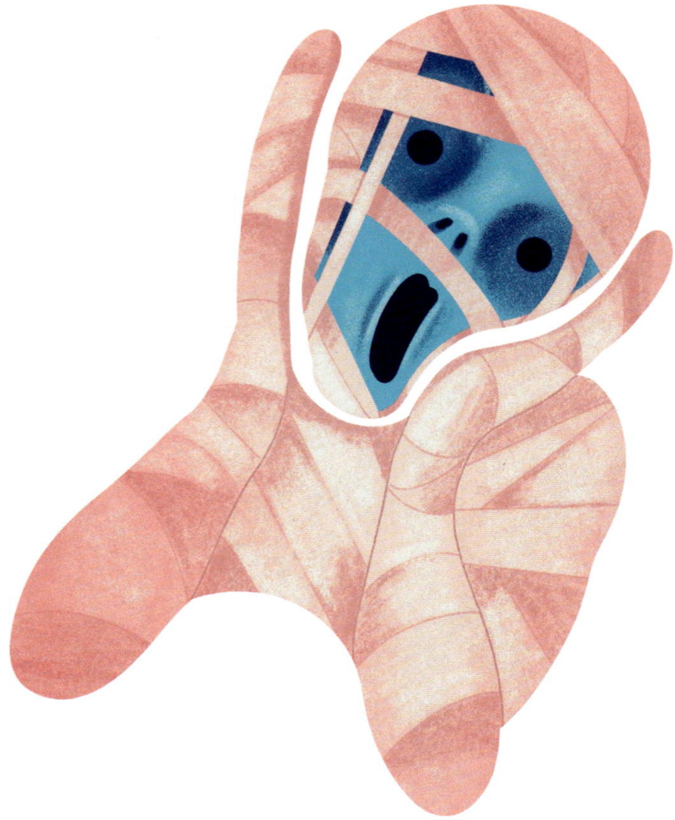

SILENT SCREAM

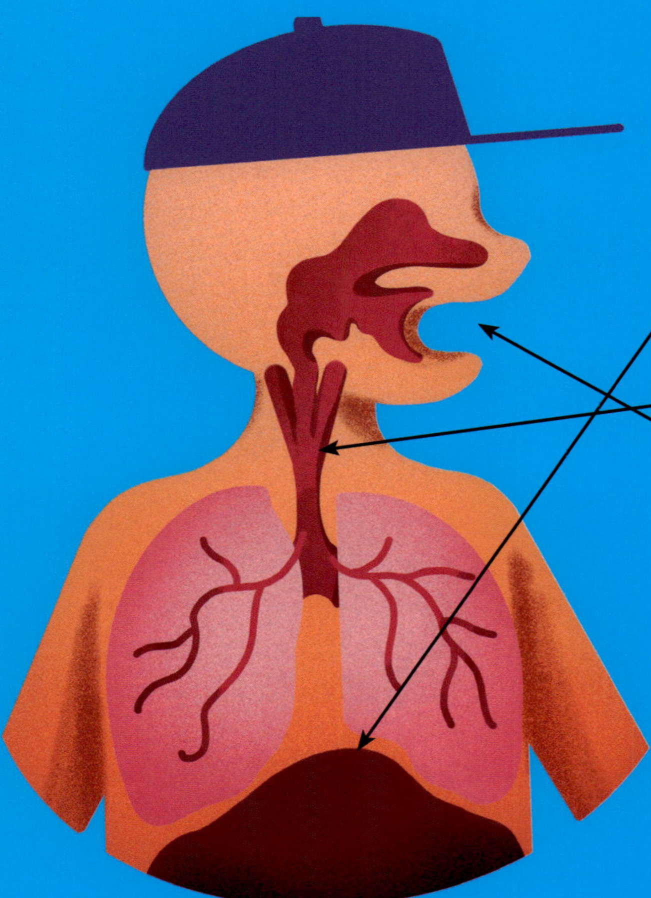

This is how your body produces sound:

1. The diaphragm muscle in the stomach pushes air through your lungs into your voicebox.
2. Flaps of skin called the vocal cords vibrate as the air passes over them.
3. The mouth, tongue, and teeth shape the vibrations to produce different sounds.

Without its stomach and lungs, the mummy would have trouble moving air out of its mouth, so no sound would come out either. It might be able to bang on a drum, but even if it managed to open its mouth, the scream would definitely be a silent one.

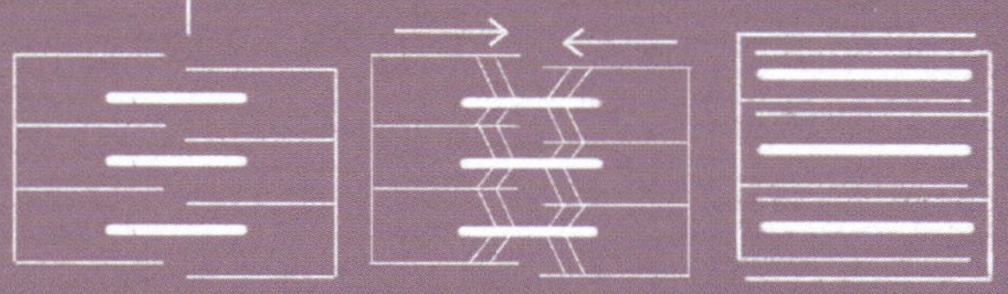

FINGER FLEXING

What about the moving and strangling bit? Well, we already know that it's the force of the muscles that causes movement in the skeleton. Every time a muscle contracts, its filaments slide past each other – think of the way people put their hands together, crossing their fingers to pray. It's called the sliding filament model. The overlapping shortens the muscle and changes the angle of the joint. That's how we are able to move body parts.

For the mummy, without moisture, its flesh would lose all its elasticity, so the filaments would be too dry to slide past one another in order to shorten the muscle. No contraction means no movement. The mummy couldn't put one foot in front of the other, let alone bend its arms at the elbows and wrap its fingers around your neck.

SOAK IT UP

Have you ever seen someone drop their phone down the toilet and have to leave it to dry out in a bag of rice? Egyptians did the same sort of thing with mummification. In moist conditions, bacteria can grow and break down the body tissue quite speedily. Embalmers beat those bacteria, saving the body from the second stage of decomposition (called putrefaction) by drying it out until it looked like a giant, human-shaped raisin. Instead of rice, they drew out the moisture with a kind of salt, called natron, stuffing it in and packing it around the dead body. After 40 days in the salt bath, the corpse would be a fraction of its former size.

A PUSHOVER

The human body is approximately 70 percent water. Muscles are 75 percent water, blood is 83 percent water, and even bones are 22 percent water. Once all that liquid had been drained from the body, a mummy would only be about a quarter of the weight of a regular human being – that's about the same as an average four-year-old! Even after a mummy had been padded out to look lifelike – using cloth, straw, and massive amounts of those linen bandages that hold it all together – would it really be a threat if it somehow got up close?

With a mummy so small and light, you could just pick it up by its feet and throw it back where it belongs – locked up in a tomb! You'd have to hope those bandages did their job, though. Its bones would be so dry and breakable from the mummification process you might find sharp shards of bone came flying off it, and you wouldn't want one of those in your eye.

You see? There's no need to worry. You're a living, breathing human being. One gentle shove from you and a mummy would be history.

mummy attack: IMPOSSIBLE!

Frankenstein's Monster

Tall and super strong with a flat head, stitches, bolts sticking out of his neck, and the sort of huge bulging forehead a Neanderthal would be proud of, this monster has a tendency towards violence – you wouldn't want to mess with it. The creature, created by the fictional character Dr. Victor Frankenstein in an attempt to defy death through science, was sewn together from dead body parts and jolted into life via the power of electricity. The monster was only a character in a story, thank goodness, but it haunted nineteenth-century readers for decades and later spawned a load of movie spin-offs.

Science vs. Fiction

Author Mary Shelley was influenced by the scientists of her day, so just how likely is it that a monster like Dr. Frankenstein's really could be built? And could it actually come to life and chase ordinary people like you?

IT'S A STITCH!

Let's start with the sewn-together body parts. In the early nineteenth century, when the book was written, the idea of attaching or reattaching a severed limb to a body seemed plain ridiculous, and it would remain impossible for nearly 150 years. Then, in 1962, after an accident in which a 12-year-old boy's right arm was ripped off (ouch!), a team of a dozen doctors managed to successfully reattach it. They began to operate on the boy within four hours of the accident, but it was a messy business.

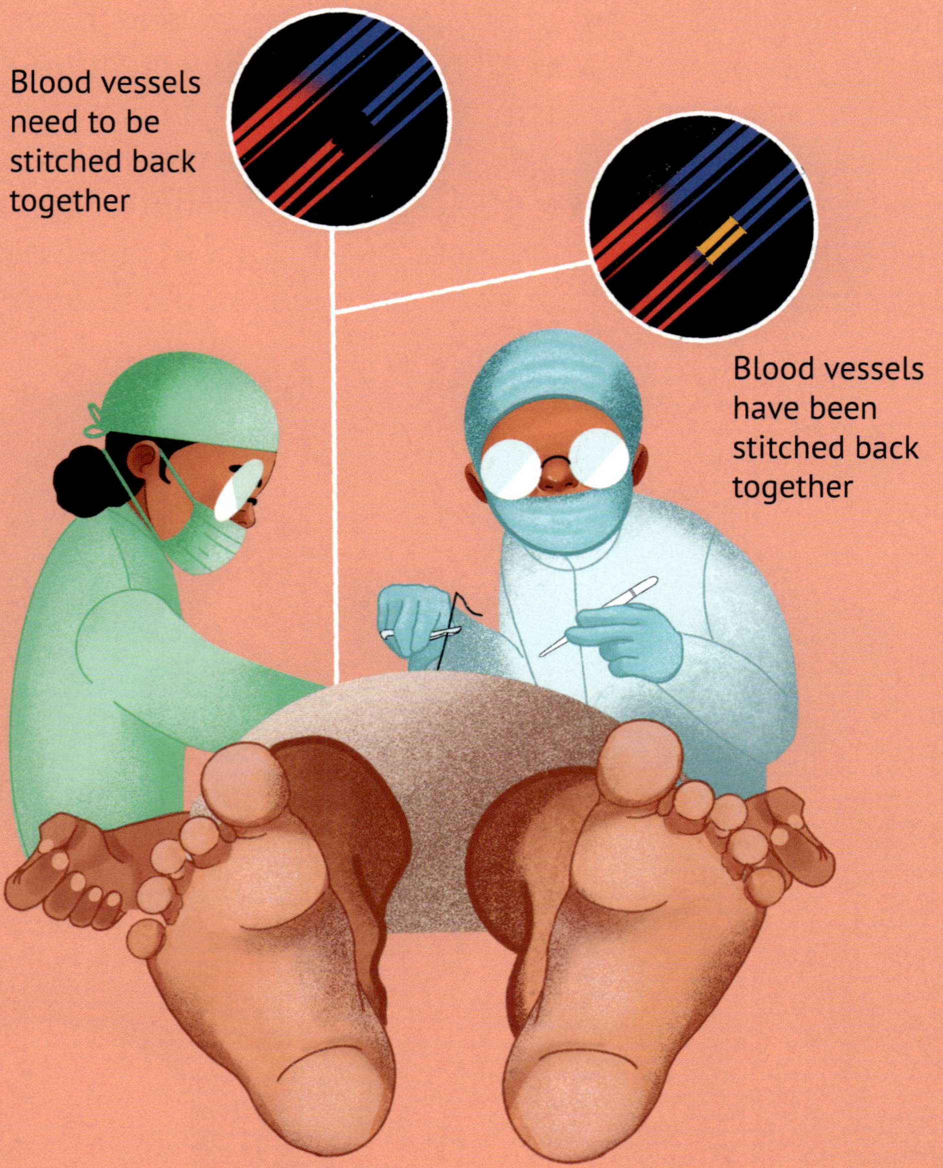

To keep the blood circulating, delivering oxygen to the cells in the arm, they had to stitch the arteries together using microsurgery. Then the veins were reattached so fluids could find their way out, stopping the arm from swelling up like a balloon. Next, several surgeries reconnected the bones, muscles, nerve bundles, and skin. A process of nerve reattachment gave the boy back the feeling in his arm and hand, but it took years of rehabilitation before he was finally able to use his right hand again. (By that time he'd learned to do all the important jobs with his left hand.)

ON THE ROCKS

Mary was right about the stitching, and even though reattachment surgery has massively improved since the 1960s, it's a lot more complicated than she imagined.

Even today, surgeons aim to reattach a severed limb within hours of an accident, and it helps if the limb is placed on ice inside a sealed bag. If too much time passes, the muscle tissue could start deteriorating or even get frostbite from direct contact with the ice.

So, attaching limbs to a torso is certainly possible, but Dr, Frankenstein would have been stitching the limb from one body to the torso of another. Can we even do that today?

A HELPING HAND

Today's surgeons can successfully transplant all sorts of body parts, usually taking a bit from a recently dead body and transferring it to someone who is living.

The first successful human heart transplant happened in 1967, but it wasn't until 2013 that French and Australian doctors performed a successful human hand and forearm transplant. These operations can work so well that the fingernails even start growing again, but that first operation took a full 13 hours.

Imagine Dr. Frankenstein working alone, attaching lots of different body parts without the state-of-the-art equipment doctors have now! The trouble is, even after the body part is attached, things can still go wrong.

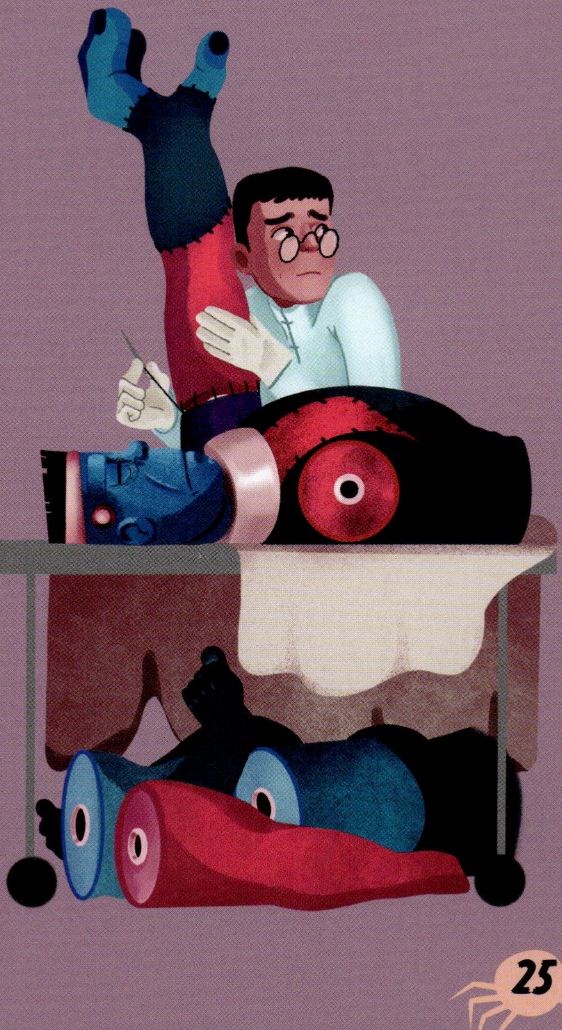

NOT YOUR TYPE

The first thing the surgeons did in reattaching the boy's arm was connect the arteries and veins to establish blood circulation. With veins and arteries belonging to different people, surgeons have to worry about just whose blood is flowing into whose arteries.

Your blood – and everyone else's, for that matter – belongs to one of four groups: A, B, AB, or O, depending on whether or not the proteins antigen A or antigen B are attached to the surface of the red blood cells. Group A has antigen A, Group B has antigen B, Group AB has both, and Group O has neither. Each group can be further divided depending on whether it contains another protein, called the RhD antigen, which makes the blood RhD+ (positive, if it has it) or RhD- (negative, if it doesn't). That means there are eight common blood types: A+, A-, B+, B-, O+, O-, AB+ and AB-. It also means that Dr. Frankenstein would have been in trouble.

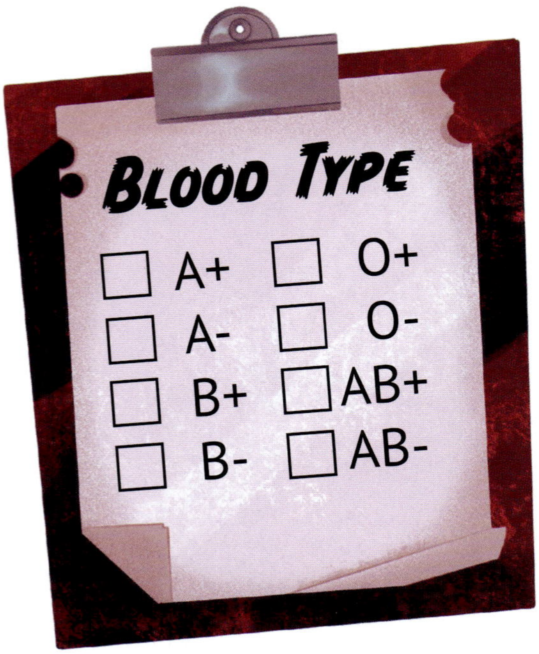

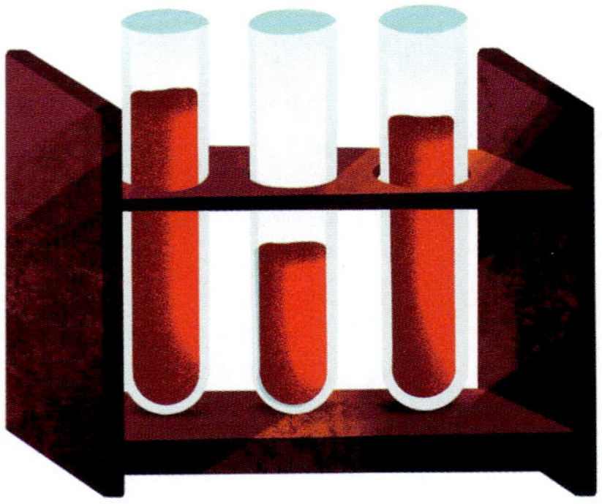

ENGINE TROUBLE

Putting the wrong sort of fuel in a car can ruin its engine, and it's kind of the same with blood groups. Mary Shelley probably knew about blood transfusions (taking blood from one person and injecting it to replace lost blood in another), because the first successful transfusion happened the year her story was published, in 1818.

The doctors performing those early transfusions couldn't understand why some operations worked and others didn't. They had no idea about the different blood groups, so it's hardly likely Dr. Frankenstein would have known either. Taking so many parts from so many different bodies, with lots of different blood groups, he'd have created one seriously messed-up monster.

GETTING ALONG

It wasn't until 1901 that the A, B, and O blood types were identified and doctors realized that they needed to follow the science to make sure blood from different bodies would get along nicely.

- People with type O- blood can donate blood to anyone, but they can only receive type O blood.
- RhD- patients can only receive RhD- blood while RhD+ patients can receive either positive or negative.
- People with type AB+ blood can only donate blood to be given to AB+ people, but they can receive blood from everyone.

So if you've got type O- blood, you are called a universal blood donor because your blood is compatible with everyone else's, whatever their blood group.

SICK MONSTERS

The chance that all of Frankenstein's monster's body parts were compatible seems remote.

When the wrong type of blood or tissue is given, the body can reject it by attacking it with antibodies. Transplant patients today are treated with immunosuppressant drugs to stop this from happening, but the monster would have had no such luck. The blood groups inside its body would have been fighting each other instead of working together to let him function as a human being. Massive and dangerous though the monster looks, his body would have been too busy attacking itself (from the inside) to even worry about attacking the likes of you.

HUMAN-BUILDING TECH

Of course, the skills and knowledge to transplant or reattach body parts do exist today, but the idea of building a monster with loads of them still seems practically impossible. In any case, for a transplant or blood transfusion to work, it's kind of helpful if the patient is alive to begin with. But could Frankenstein have brought his weird collection of body parts back to life with the help of electricity?

BACK FROM THE DEAD

Mary Shelley knew about experiments where scientists passed an electric current through the bodies of recently dead animals, while spectators watched amazed and revolted as the creature's muscles contracted. A similar experiment was performed on the corpse of a prisoner who had just been executed, and observers were horrified to witness the muscles on the deceased person's face quivering and contorting. According to one report, one of the dead man's eyes opened during the procedure, just as if he were coming back to life! Scary stuff!

GETTING THE MESSAGE

However, muscles do not have minds of their own. They need a stimulus or message from a nerve cell ordering them to contract. For your foot to kick a ball, your brain has to send electrical messages to motor neurons in your leg, which then stimulate muscle fibers in your leg to contract, causing your leg to pull back and kick forward.

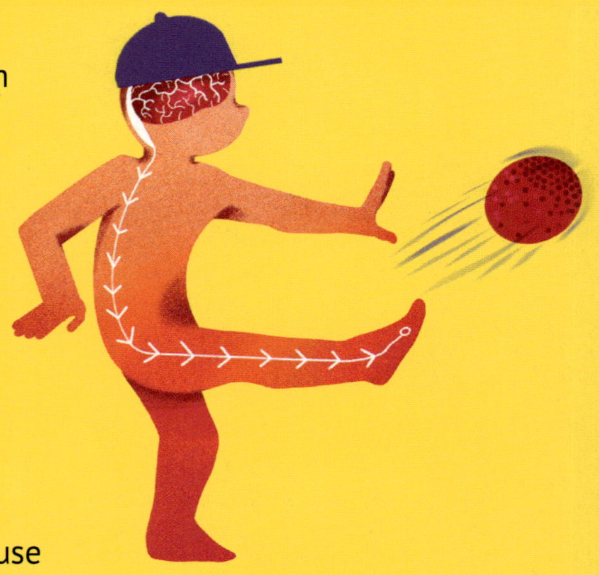

Those early scientists noticed that passing electric currents through recently deceased animals could lead to their muscles contracting, but in reality the muscles were just confusing the electricity with electric messages they used to receive from the brain when they were alive. Unfortunately for Dr. Frankenstein, once the body tissue degenerates and the nerve cells die, the electricity won't cause those muscles to contract anymore. The only way to keep those cells alive is to attach them to a compatible host who is alive. Since Dr. Frankenstein's creature is made up of dead parts, those parts would most certainly stay dead.

Okay, it doesn't seem likely that Frankenstein would have been able to reanimate his monster using electricity, but maybe there are other ways?

CLEVER CELLS

Some film versions of Frankenstein suggest that one modern-day solution to bringing the monster to life might be through the use of stem cells. So just what are stem cells and why are they so special? They are cells in a very early stage of development of human life, soon after the sperm meets the egg. They are special because they can develop into any other type of cell, such as blood cells, bone cells, or brain cells.

Scientific studies suggest many ways of using stem cells to cure diseases. However, using them can be about as controversial as Frankenstein's monster was in the nineteenth century.

With new medical discoveries, doctors will be able to help many more injured or ill people, but why would they ever want to give life to a sewn-up creature made up of various dead human parts anyway?

1. Egg and sperm
2. Fertilized egg developing stem cells
3. Stem cells that go on to develop into brain and heart cells
4. Human baby (9 months later)

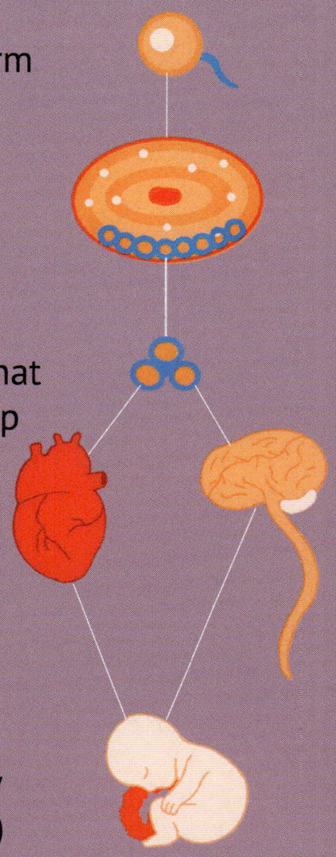

MAN OR MACHINE?

If Mary Shelley was alive today,and she wanted to reimagine her horror story twenty-first-century-style, she'd be well advised to opt for a cyborg, combining machine and human parts. Today, a recently stopped heart can be restarted using electric shocks and a severed arm can be reattached or replaced with a high-functioning machine limb. People can have implants to improve their hearing and wearable technology can enhance our brainpower or strength. The technology is there and always improving – let's hope it continues to be used to improve people's lives rather than to make monsters!

Luckily, it seems unlikely we'll ever meet the monster Mary Shelley originally imagined, but if one ever did come to life, remember: it's probably suffering far more pain than it could ever inflict on you.

Frankenstein's monster:
IMPOSSIBLE!

GLOSSARY

afterlife ancient Egyptians believed that after death there was a never-ending perfect life waiting for them

airways in the human body, the passages from the nose and mouth to the lungs

ancient Egyptians the people who lived near the River Nile from around 3000 BCE to about 30 CE

antibody a substance (protein) produced by white blood cells to fight infections

antigen a substance (usually a protein) that causes the immune system to produce antibodies (see above)

apocalypse the end of the world

artery a blood vessel that carries blood from the heart

bacteria tiny living things

beef jerky a sundried strip of beef

blood vessel a tube that carries blood around the body

brittle hard, but easy to break

canopic jar a stone or pottery container for storing body organs during the mummification process

cell one of the tiny building blocks that make up all living things

chemical a substance produced or used in a reaction between two or more substances

climate the usual weather for an area

corpse a dead body

cyborg a creature that is part human, part machine

decay/decompose to slowly break down after death

deteriorate to become worse

digestive system the organs inside the body, including the mouth, stomach, liver and intestines, that digest food

dilate to widen or open up

embalmer someone whose job it is to preserve dead bodies

enzyme a substance that is produced by a living thing that helps make a chemical change happen, such as digesting food to release the nutrients

frostbite damage to skin and body tissues caused by very cold temperatures

fungus a living thing that is similar to a plant and feeds on dead or rotting plants and animals

immunosuppressant a drug that stops the body's immune system from reacting, for instance, against a transplanted organ

inanimate not alive

linen a type of fabric made from flax

moisture very tiny drops of water

muscle filament a thin thread of muscle fiber

nerve one of the long fibers that carries messages between the brain and other parts of the body

organ a body part, such as a heart, kidney, or brain

phenomenon an event or fact

preservation keeping something in good condition

reanimate to give something new life or energy

sarcophagus a stone coffin

Shelley, Mary (1797–1851) English novelist who wrote *Frankenstein*

spore a tiny cell that will develop into a new plant or fungi

tendon a strong band of body tissue that ties a muscle to a bone

tomb a large grave for burial, especially one that is aboveground

vein a blood vessel that carries blood to the heart

virus a tiny living thing that causes diseases in people, other animals, and plants

vocal cords the flaps of tissue in the throat that vibrate (move side to side) to produce the voice

Voodoo (or Vodou) a form of religion using magic practiced by many in and around Haiti

FURTHER INFORMATION

Further freaky science reading:

The Bright and Bold Human Body
by Izzi Howell and Sonya Newland
(Wayland, 2019)
The books in the series include:
The Digestive System
The Heart, Lungs and Blood
The Brain and Nervous System
The Reproductive System
The Skeleton and Muscles
The Senses

Cause, Effect and Chaos in the Human Body
by Paul Mason
(Wayland, 2020)

A Question of Science: Why Don't Your Eyeballs Fall Out? And Other Questions About the Human Body
by Anna Claybourne
(Wayland, 2020)

BOOM Science: Human Body
by Georgia Amson-Bradshaw
(PowerKids Press, 2020)

100% Get the Whole Picture: Human Body
by Paul Mason
(Cavendish Square, 2024)

Places to see freaky science up close:

American Museum of Natural History
200 Central Park West
New York, NY 10024
https://www.amnh.org

National Museum of Natural History
10th Street and Constitution Avenue NW
Washington, DC 20560
https:/naturalhistory.si.edu

Natural History Museum
900 Exposition Boulevard
Los Angeles, CA 90007
https://nhm.org

Canada Museum of Nature
240 McLeod Street
Ottawa, ON K2P 2R1
https://nature.ca/en/

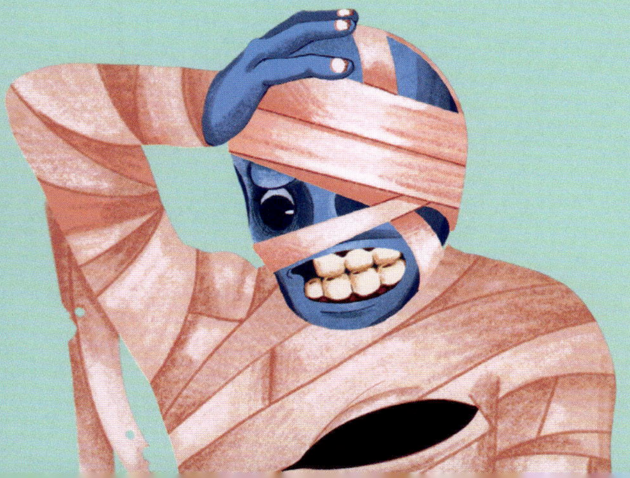

INDEX